HORRIBLE HABITATS
Streets and Alleys

Sharon Katz Cooper

Raintree

Chicago, Illinois

www.heinemannraintree.com
Visit our website to find out
more information about
Heinemann-Raintree books.

To order:
☎ Phone 888-454-2279
⌨ Visit www.heinemannraintree.com
to browse our catalog and order online.

Edited by Charlotte Guillain, Rebecca Rissman, and
Sian Smith
Designed by Joanna Hinton-Malivoire
Picture research by Tracy Cummins and
Heather Mauldin
Originated by Chroma Graphics (Overseas) Pte. Ltd
Printed and bound in China by CTPS

14 13 12 11 10
10 9 8 7 6 5 4 3 2

**Library of Congress Cataloging-in-Publication
Data**
Katz Cooper, Sharon.
Streets and alleys / Sharon Katz Cooper.
p. cm. -- (Horrible habitats)
Includes bibliographical references and index.
ISBN 978-1-4109-3491-8 (hc)
ISBN 978-1-4109-3499-4 (pb)
1. Urban ecology (Biology)--Juvenile literature. 2.
Urban pests--Habitat--Juvenile literature. 3. Streets--
Juvenile literature. 4. Alleys--Juvenile literature. I. Title.
QH541.5.C6K3823 2009
577.5'6--dc22
                                      2009002593

Acknowledgments
The author and publisher are grateful to the following
for permission to reproduce copyright material:
Age Fotostock p. **20** (© Danilo Donadoni); Alamy pp.
13 (© Don Vail), **18** (© Corbis Premium RF/DLILLC),
25 (© Frances M. Roberts), **26** (© dumbandmad.com);
Corbis p. **22** (© Bob Sacha); DRK Photo p. **21**
(© Martin Harvey); Getty Images pp. **7** (© Allan
McPhail), **9** (© John Downer); Derek Jensen p. **16**;
Minden p. **11** (© Cyril Ruoso); Photolibrary pp. **8**
(© Tony Tilford), **10** (© EA. Janes), **12** (© Robin
Redfern), **17** (© Juniors Bildarchiv), **19** (© DesignPics
Inc.), **23** (© Bartomeu Borrell); Shutterstock pp. **4**
(© Brian J. Abela), **5** (© Junker), **6** (© Dmitry Remesov),
14 (© Pallando), **15** (© Gastón M. Charles), **24**
(© Tobias Machhaus), **27** (© Glenda M. Powers), **28a**
(© Keith Levit), **28b** (© Stephan Glebowski), **28c**
(© Alex James Bramwell), **29d** (© cbpix), **29e**
(© Serghei Starus), **29f** (© Bruce MacQueen)

Cover photograph of pigeons reproduced with
permission of Alamy (© Simon De Glanville].

Every effort has been made to contact copyright
holders of any material reproduced in this book. Any
omissions will be rectified in subsequent printings if
notice is given to the publisher.

All the Internet addresses (URLs) given in this book
were valid at the time of going to press. However, due
to the dynamic nature of the Internet, some addresses
may have changed, or sites may have changed or
ceased to exist since publication. While the author and
publisher regret any inconvenience this may cause
readers, no responsibility for any such changes can be
accepted by either the author or the publisher.

Some words are shown in bold, **like this.** You can find
out what they mean by looking in the glossary.

Contents

What Is a Habitat?

A **habitat** is a place where plants and animals can find what they need to live. Like you, they need food, water, and shelter.

squirrel

5

There are many types of **habitats**. Forests, ponds, and fields are all habitats. But even a street can be a habitat.

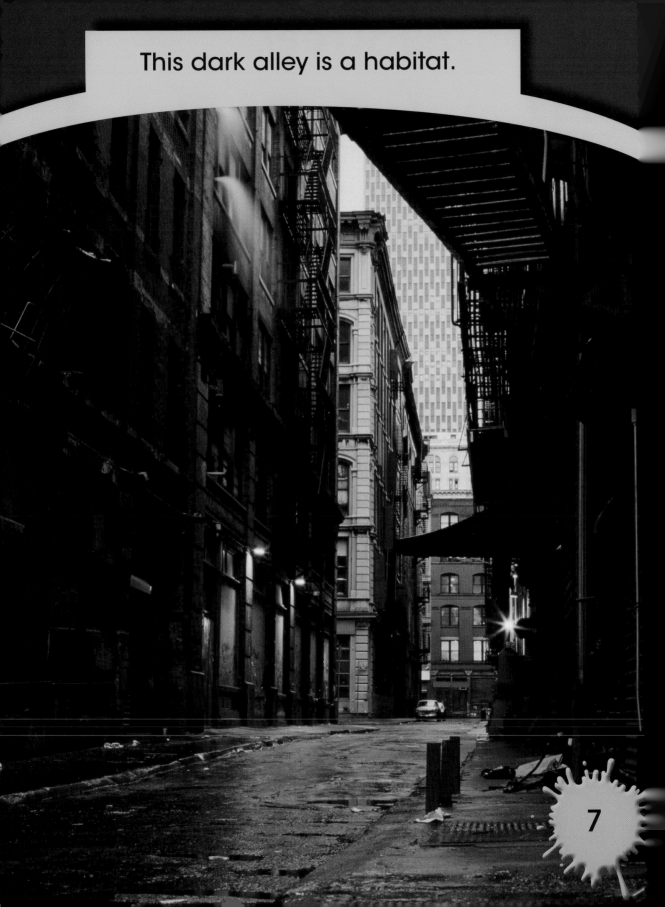

This dark alley is a habitat.

7

Out on the Street

Rats are common street animals. They live close to humans because people leave old food and yummy trash for them to eat.

Rats will eat moldy or rotting food.

FUN FACT

A group of rats is called a **mischief**.

Rats **urinate,** or pee, as they run around. This leaves a trail that other rats can follow. We can't see these trails in the dark, but other rats can smell them!

FUN FACT

Rats go to trash cans at night for a delicious snack. They sometimes find dog poo there to munch on.

A street could hold thousands of rats because they make babies very quickly. One female can have three to six **litters**, or sets, of babies a year. Each litter could have at least 12 babies.

rat babies

Rats can carry many **diseases**.
Diseases can make people ill or
die.

Hair for Dinner

Stray, or homeless, cats wander around alleys. They eat rats. They also spend a lot of time licking their own hair to stay clean. They swallow some of that hair.

A cat's tongue is rough. This helps the cat to clean itself.

Hair Vomit!

Swallowing hair is a problem for cats. They can't **digest** it, or break it down, so it forms clumps in their stomachs. Then they vomit it out. Yum – hairballs!

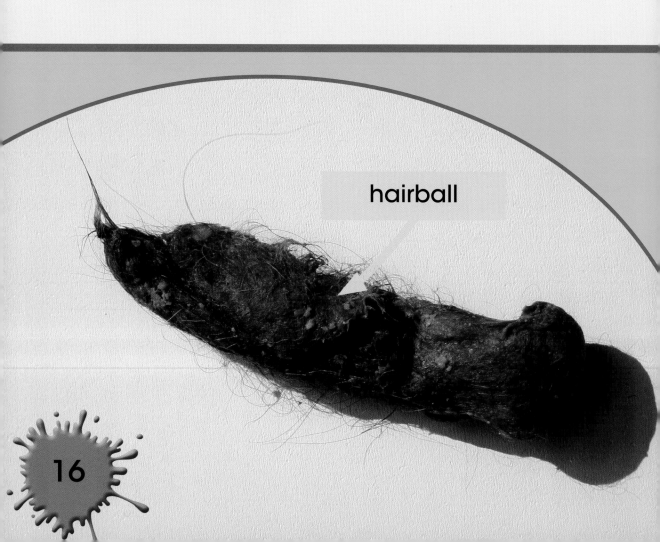

hairball

Rabid Raccoons

In some places, raccoons slink around alleys. They are good climbers. They climb over fences and up the sides of trash cans looking for food.

Raccoons use their own pee and poo to mark the places they think of as their own. These places are called **territories**.

NOT-SO-FUN FACT

Some raccoons carry the **disease**, or illness, rabies. So if you see a raccoon, stay away!

Roaches' Favorite Places

Cockroaches are famous street creatures. They live in sewers during the day. At night they scurry into the street to look for better food.

Cockroaches don't like the light. They prefer dark places like this hole.

Cockroaches eat rotting food and human poo. They also eat grease from stoves and glue under the labels of cans. They even eat fingernails and hair from people!

In this roach poo you can see some of the things the roach has eaten.

23

Scavenging Birds

You may see many birds in city streets. Some birds such as crows and seagulls are **scavengers**. This means they will eat what they can find. They will even eat bits of other dead birds.

This crow is eating a dead pigeon.

Large numbers of pigeons live in city streets, too. Pigeons eat almost anything, including rotting food.

Hungry Squirrels

Squirrels run and jump all over streets and lawns. They eat seeds and nuts. They will also poke around through trash bags for leftover human food, bugs, and even dead animals.

Squirrels chew on branches to sharpen and clean their teeth. They chew on power lines for the same reason. Sometimes this causes the power to go out in nearby houses.

If they can find French fries, street squirrels will eat these too.

Street Matching

Which of these animals would you not find in the streets? Note: not all of these animals are in this book.

d

e

f

Glossary

digest break down food into small pieces that the body can use. Animals usually digest things in their stomachs.

disease illness

habitat place where plants and animals live and grow

litter group of babies born at the same time

mischief group of rats

scavenger bird or other animal that feeds on waste and other dead animals

stray animal without a home

territory area that an animal thinks of as its own

urinate pee

Find Out More

Find out

Why is the rhinoceros cockroach famous?

Books to Read

Dickmann, Nancy. *Cockroaches.* Chicago: Raintree, 2005.

Marrin, Albert. *Oh Rats! The Story of Rats and People.* New York: Dutton Juvenile, 2006.

Websites

http://www.nature.ca/notebooks/english/brnrat.htm
Learn about rats and see pictures of them here.

http://www.nhm.ac.uk/kids-only/life/life-small/cockroaches/
Find out some fascinating facts about cockroaches on this Website.

http://www.birds.cornell.edu/pigeonwatch
At this site, you can learn about pigeons and sign up to observe them.

31

Index